Bible-Based
Word Games
Primary

By

Linda Standke

Cover illustration by

Darcy Bell-Myers

Inside illustrations by

Julie Anderson

Publishers

In Celebration™

a division of Instructional Fair • TS Denison

Grand Rapids, Michigan 49544

Credits:
Author: Linda Standke
Project Director/Editor: Sherrill B. Flora
Cover Illustrator: Darcy Bell-Myers
Inside Illustrations: Julie Anderson
Graphic Designer: Deborah Hanson McNiff

About the Author
Linda Standke lives in Bloomington, Minnesota with her husband Bill and their four sons. Being an active member in her church, Linda has served on the Christian Education Committee, directed Preschool Bible School, conducted Preschool Music, teaches Sunday School, and was employed as the Coordinator of Children's Ministries. Writing educational material is something Linda says, "Is truly a blessing in my life. To be spreading God's message through my books is fulfilling a dream and an answer to prayer."

Standard Book Number: 1-56822-319-6
SPCN: 990-219-2254
Bible-Based Word Games—Primary
Copyright © 1996 by In Celebration™
a division of Instructional Fair • TS Denison
2400 Turner Avenue NW
Grand Rapids, Michigan 49544

All Rights Reserved • Printed in the USA

Table of Contents

The Flood

During the flood God stayed with Noah and kept him safe.
God is always with you, too. Fill in the crossword puzzle below.

1. rain
2. rainbow
3. promise
4. Noah
5. animals
6. flood

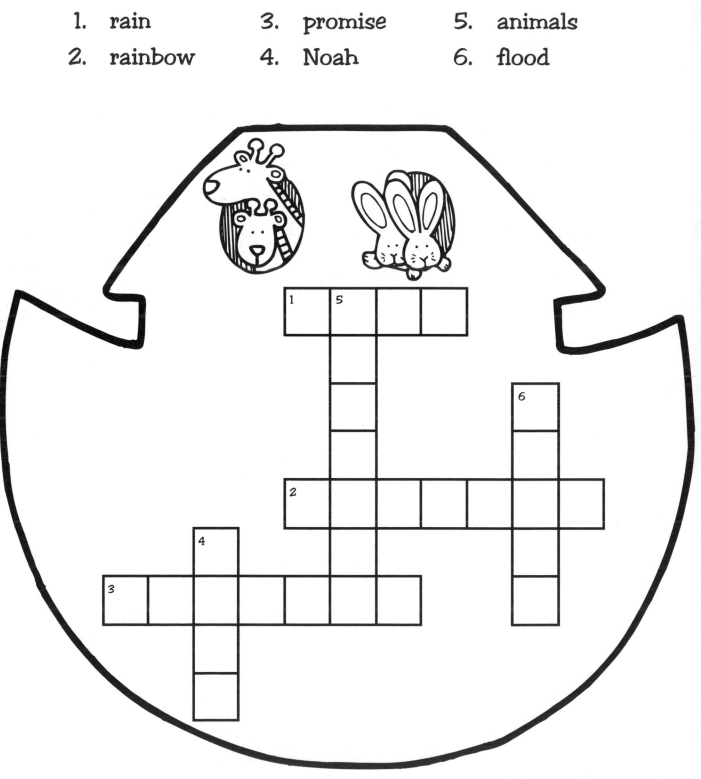

God's Promise

God gave us a promise that He will never flood the earth again.
Connect the dots and discover the beautiful image of God's promise.

IF9540 *Bible-Based Word Games—Primary*

10 Plagues

Pharaoh would not let Moses and the Israelites leave Egypt!
So, God sent ten plagues upon the people.
Find and circle the ten plagues listed below in the puzzle.

BLOOD FROGS GNATS FLIES LIVESTOCK
BOILS HAIL LOCUSTS DARKNESS FIRSTBORN

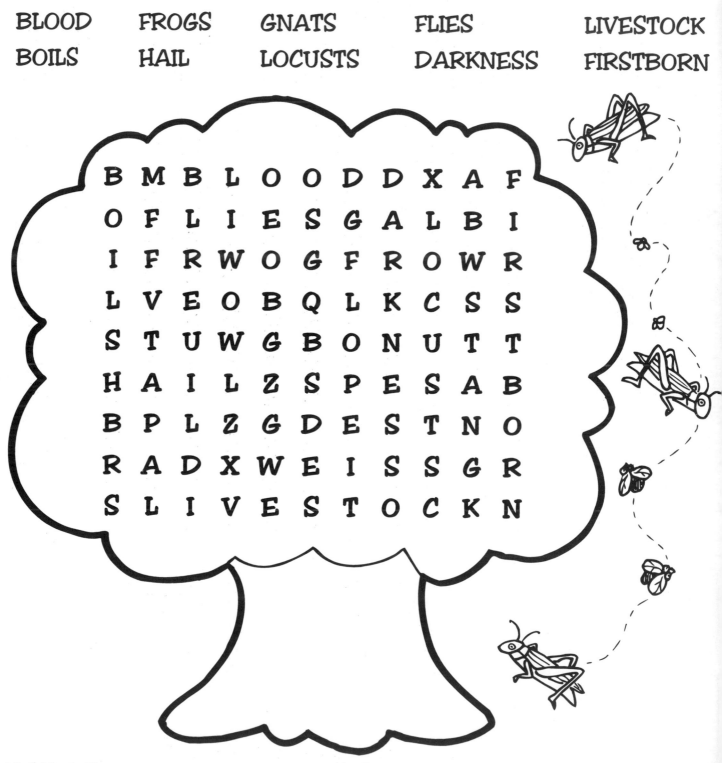

```
B M B L O O D D X A F
O F L I E S G A L B I
I F R W O G F R O W R
L V E O B Q L K C S S
S T U W G B O N U T T
H A I L Z S P E S A B
B P L Z G D E S T N O
R A D X W E I S S G R
S L I V E S T O C K N
```

IF9540 Bible-Based Word Games—Primar

Moses brought the commandments down from Mount Sinai.

Can you decode the first two commandments using the letter key below?

Left tablet (Exodus 20:2 NIV):

"__
1

__ __
4 11

__ __ __
9 10 3

__ __ __ __
12 5 7 13

__ __ __ __
8 5 2 7

__ __ __, ..."
6 5 13

Exodus 20:2 NIV

Right tablet (Exodus 20:3 NIV):

"__ __ __
8 5 2

__ __ __ __ __
14 10 4 12 12

__ __ __ __
10 4 15 3

__ __
16 5

__ __ __ __ __
5 9 10 3 7

__ __ __ __
6 5 13 14

__ __ __ __ __ __
16 3 17 5 7 3

__ __."
11 3

Exodus 20:3 NIV

A	B	D	E	F	G	H	I	L	M	N	O	R	S	T	U	V	Y
4	16	13	3	17	6	10	1	12	11	16	5	7	14	9	2	15	8

7

IF9540 Bible-Based Word Games—Primary

Match the Stories

Match the people from the Bible with the correct picture.

Praise God!

Start with the P and write each letter in the spaces below as you come to them in the maze.

P _ _ _ _ _ _ _ _ _ _ _ _ _ _ _ _ _ _ _.

God is With You

Joshua struggled just like we do at times. What were God's comforting words to him? We can use these words in our lives today.

H_V_   _ N_T
C _ MM _ ND _ D   Y _ _ ?
B _   STR _ NG   _ ND
C _ _ R _ G _ _ _ S....TH _
L _ RD   Y _ _ R   G _ D   W _ LL
B _   W _ TH   Y _ _
WH _ R _ V _ R   Y _ _   G _ .

Joshua 1:9 NIV

A   E   I   O   U

Fill in the missing vowels using the code to read the Bible verse.

IF9540 *Bible-Based Word Games—Primary*

God is Awesome

Our God is an awesome God! How are we to stand before him?

Ecclesiastes 5:1 NIV tell us.

Color each of the squares that have a ▲ in the corner.

The Bible verse will appear for you to read.

▲	■	●	■	●	■	●	■	●	■	▲
S	T	H	E	R	E	F	O	R	E	B

▲	▲	▲	▲	●	■	●	■	●	▲	▲
G	H	I	R	S	T	A	N	D	S	U

▲	▲	■	●	▲	▲	▲	▲	▲	▲	▲
D	O	I	N	T	K	M	N	P	R	T

▲	▲	▲	■	●	■	▲	▲	▲	▲	▲
B	D	F	A	W	E	H	J	L	P	Z

▲	●	■	▲	▲	▲	▲	▲	▲	▲	▲
Y	O	F	X	N	W	Y	P	D	G	J

▲	▲	▲	▲	▲	▲	●	■	●	▲	▲
P	L	D	C	A	F	G	O	D	B	Q

PSALM 23

In the puzzle below, find and circle the familiar words of the 23rd Psalm.
Remember the words are backwards, across, and up and down.

Words to find:

The Lord is

my shepherd.

Psalm 23

```
S R Q L U V 3
H B L O R D 2
E W X A B F M
P G J M N T L
H S V R T H A
E D F H J E S
R A S I K M P
D C L P M Y Q
```

IF9540 *Bible-Based Word Games—Primary*

3 Jews

King Nebuchadnezzar wanted people to worship false gods.
Three Jews refused because they loved God.
Decode their names below.

A B C D E G H M N O R S

© In Celebration™   IF9540 *Bible-Based Word Games—Primary*

BAPTISM

God was very pleased with Jesus. When John baptized Jesus something very special happened. Beginning with the letter "H", go around the dove and write every other letter on the spaces provided.

START

_ _

_ _ _ _ _ _

_ _ _ _ _

_ _ _ _ _ _ _ _ _

_ _ _ _ _ _ _

_ _ _ _ _

_

_ _ _ _

_ _ _ _ _ _ _ _

_ _ : _ _ _

God Can Do

Many people wonder what God can really do.
What does Luke teach us about God?

Decode the message below to find out what the Bible says God can do.

___ ___ ___   ___ ___ ___
 8   2   3   6   9   4

___ ___
 3   2

___ ___ ___ ___ ___ ___ ___ ___ ___ ___
 5   0   5   1 11 10   7 12   4   8

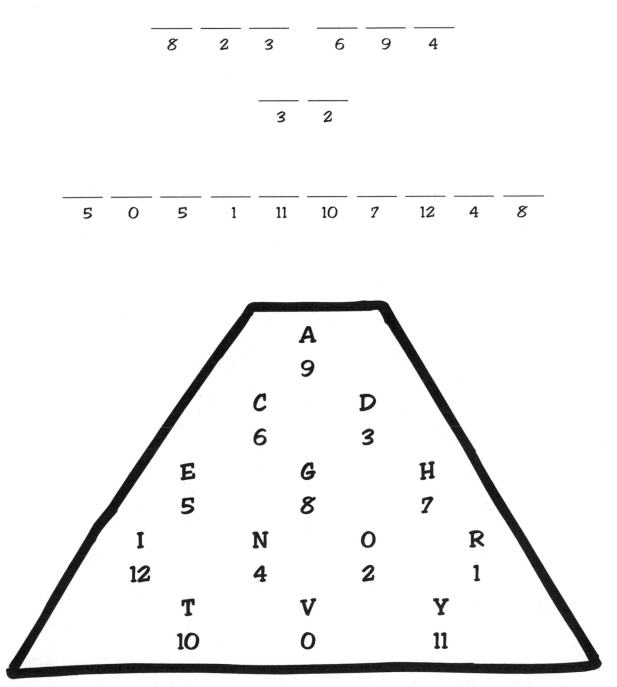

A 9

C 6   D 3

E 5   G 8   H 7

I 12   N 4   O 2   R 1

T 10   V 0   Y 11

Friendship

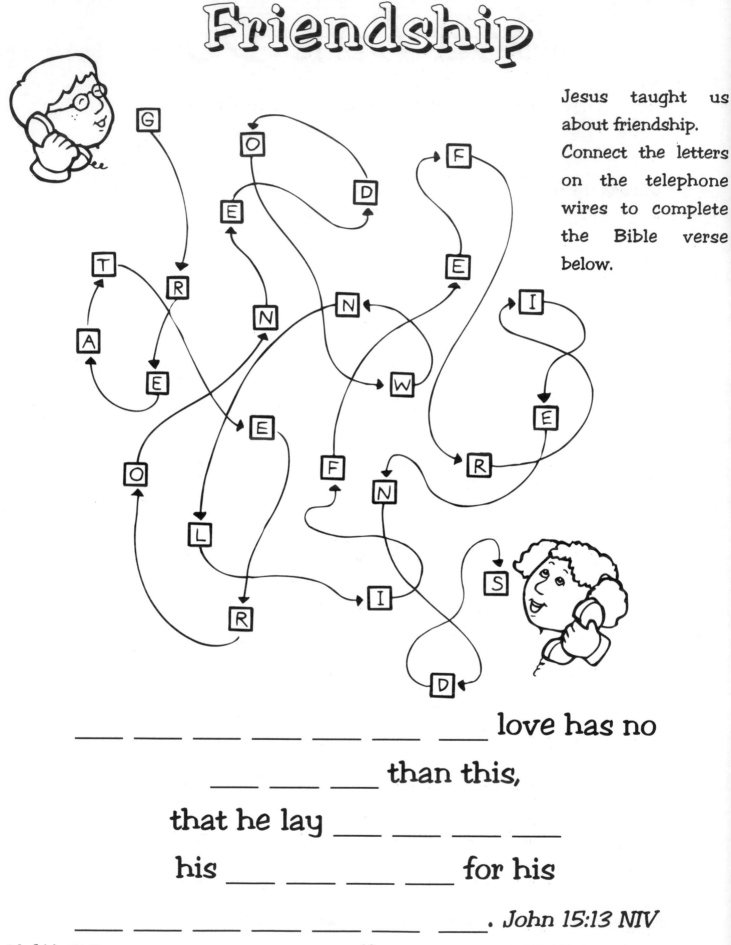

Jesus taught us about friendship. Connect the letters on the telephone wires to complete the Bible verse below.

__ __ __ __ __ __ love has no

__ __ __ than this,

that he lay __ __ __ __

his __ __ __ __ __ for his

__ __ __ __ __ __ __. *John 15:13 NIV*

Fishing for Men

Jesus taught his disciples about the importance of believing in God.
What did Jesus say when he asked them to be disciples?
Catch the fish in order and write the words in the spaces.

"_ _ _ _ _ , _ _ _ _ _ _ _ _ _ _ ,...

_ _ _ _ _ _ _ _ _ _ _ _ _

_ _ _ _ _ _ _ _ _ _ _ _ _ _ _ ."

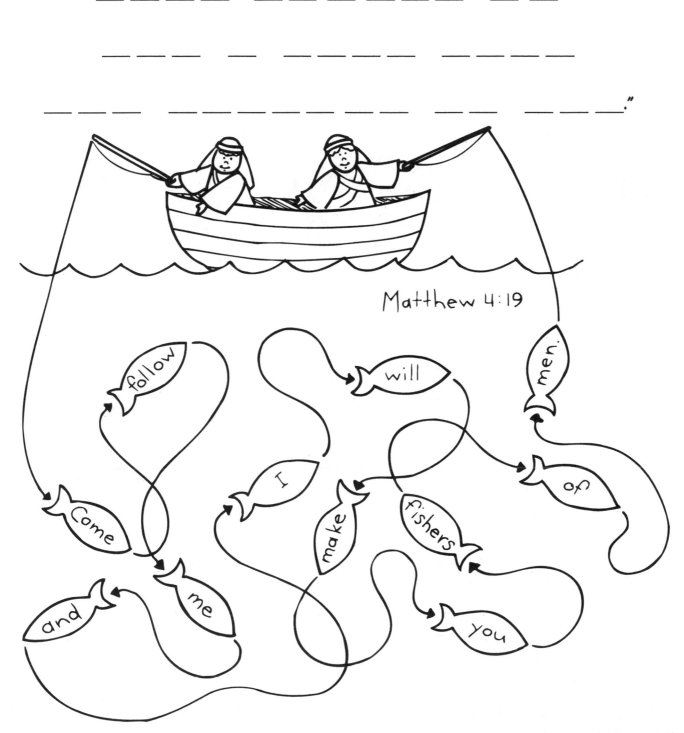

Matthew 4:19

(fish words: follow, will, men, Come, I, make, fishers, of, and, me, you)

New Creation

2 Corinthians 5:17 NIV: Therefore, if anyone is in Christ,
he is a new creation; the old has gone, the new has come!

Starting at the caterpillar, find your way through the maze.

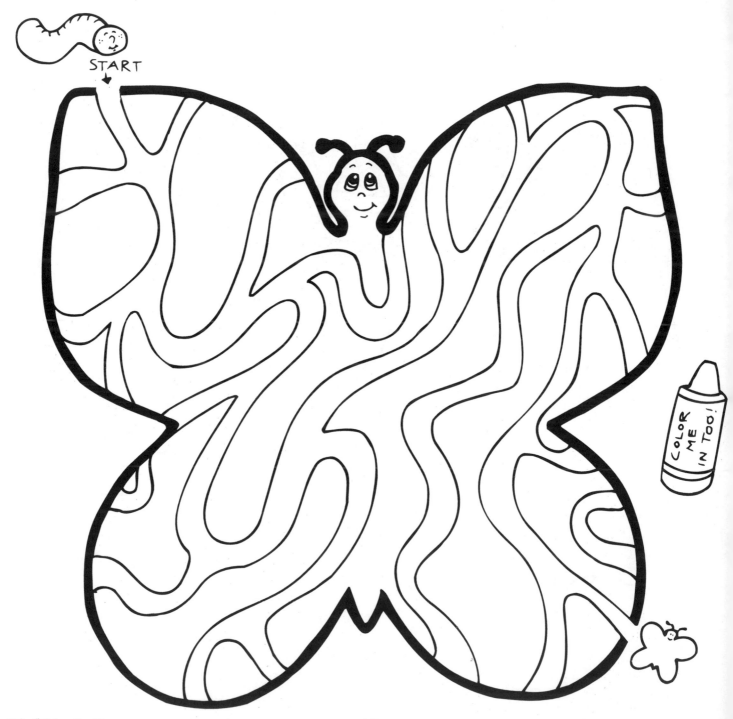

START

COLOR ME IN TOO!

Galatians 5:22

But the fruit of the spirit is
LOVE, JOY, PEACE, PATIENCE, KINDNESS, GOODNESS,
FAITHFULNESS, GENTLENESS and SELF-CONTROL.

Paul tells us how to live in the Spirit of God.

Fill in the Fruits of the Spirit from the verse above in the spaces below.

Matthew 4:10

Decode the following Bible verse.

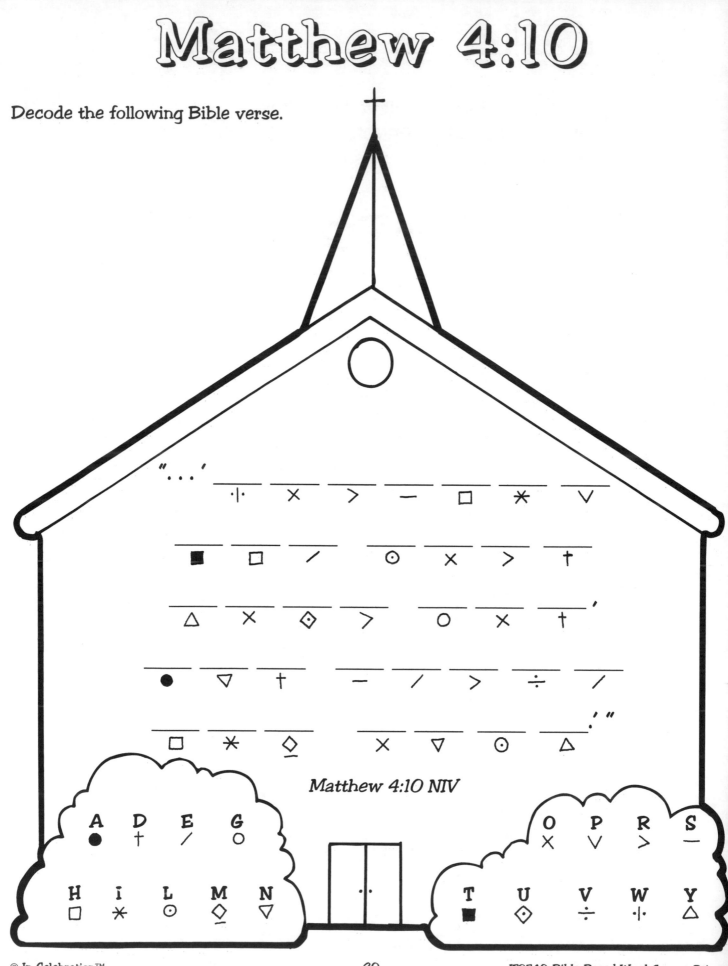

Matthew 4:10 NIV

A ●	D †	E /	G ○
H □	I ✳	L ⊙	M ◇	N ▽

O ✕	P ∨	R >	S —
T ■	U ◈	V ÷	W ·|·	Y △

IF9540 *Bible-Based Word Games—Primar*

Love

Jesus teaches us many things.
One command He gave was:

John 13:34 NIV

Use this key to
fill in the letters.

A E H L N O R T V

Ask, Seek, Knock

Jesus said,

" ___ ___ ___ and it will

be given to you;

___ ___ ___ ___ and you will

find; ___ ___ ___ ___ ___ ___

and the door will be

___ ___ ___ ___ to you."

Matthew 7:7 NIV

Fill in the missing words from the Bible verse above.

Use the words below to help you.

seek, knock, ask, open

Be Saved

Each word of the Bible verse below is hidden three times in this puzzle.
Can you circle each of the words three times?
The words may be hidden diagonally, backwards, across, up and down.

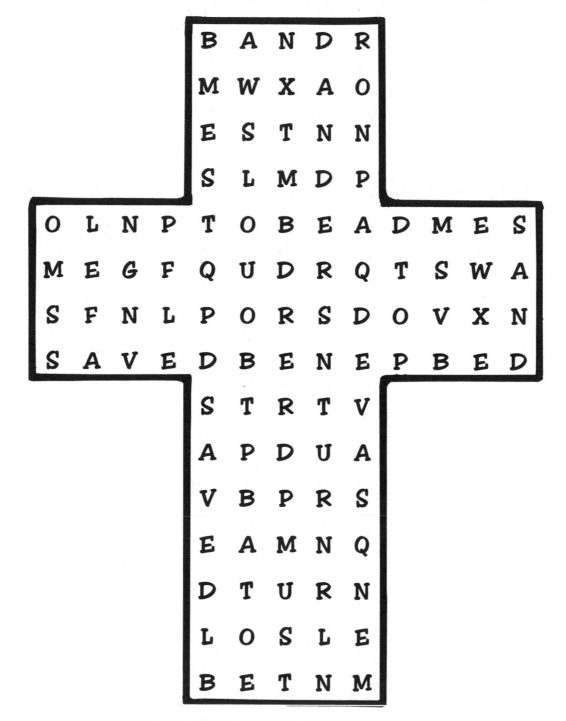

```
          B  A  N  D  R
          M  W  X  A  O
          E  S  T  N  N
          S  L  M  D  P
O  L  N  P  T  O  B  E  A  D  M  E  S
M  E  G  F  Q  U  D  R  Q  T  S  W  A
S  F  N  L  P  O  R  S  D  O  V  X  N
S  A  V  E  D  B  E  N  E  P  B  E  D
          S  T  R  T  V
          A  P  D  U  A
          V  B  P  R  S
          E  A  M  N  Q
          D  T  U  R  N
          L  O  S  L  E
          B  E  T  N  M
```

"Turn to me and be saved, . . ."

Isaiah 45:22 NIV

Rejoice Again and Again!

Rejoice in the Lord always.
Philippians 4:4 NIV

How many times can you find the word **REJOICE**?
Circle the word as you find it.

R E J O I C E F D R
B R D J O L R R R E
R E J O I C E E C J
H J Q F G N J J B O
K O B N P O O O N I
L I U M I P I I M C
P C S C T S C C U E
Q E E S M N E E P S

Let Others See Jesus in You

Jesus wants us to tell others about Him.
Decode the Bible verse below.

"YOU ARE THE LIGHT OF THE WORLD."

Matthew 5:14 NIV

A ♡ D ⬖ E ✝ F 🌷 G △ H ☽ I ❀ L ✺ O ⬠ R ◯ T ▭ U ▢ Y ✳ W ☆

Jesus Loves Me

This familiar song is the key to completing this crossword puzzle.
Use the missing words from the song to complete the puzzle.

Jesus loves me this I _____ (5)

For the Bible tells me _____ (6)

Little ones to Him _____ (1 down)

They are weak, but He is _____ (7)

Yes, _____ loves me (3)

Yes, Jesus _____ me (2)

Yes, Jesus loves _____ (4)

The _____ tells me so (1 across)

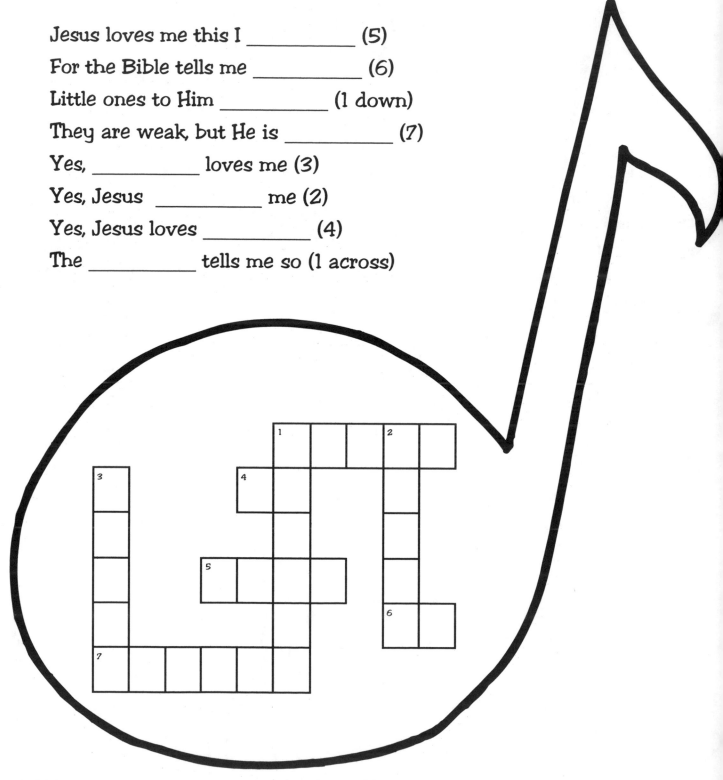

Talk to God

Wherever you are or whatever you are doing, you can always talk to God.
Beginning at the arrow, write every other letter on the spaces below.

START

— ——— ———— ———

———— ——— ———

——— ——— .

My Heart Belongs to Jesus

To find the message, start with the letter "G" and follow the maze through the heart.
Write each letter as you come to them on the spaces below.

____ ____ ____ ____ ____ ____ ____ ____ ____ ____ ____ ____

____ ____ ____ ____ ____ ____ ____ ____ ____ ____ ____ .

Serve Each Other

Pick up the words as you go through the maze.
Write them in order on the spaces below to complete the Bible verse.

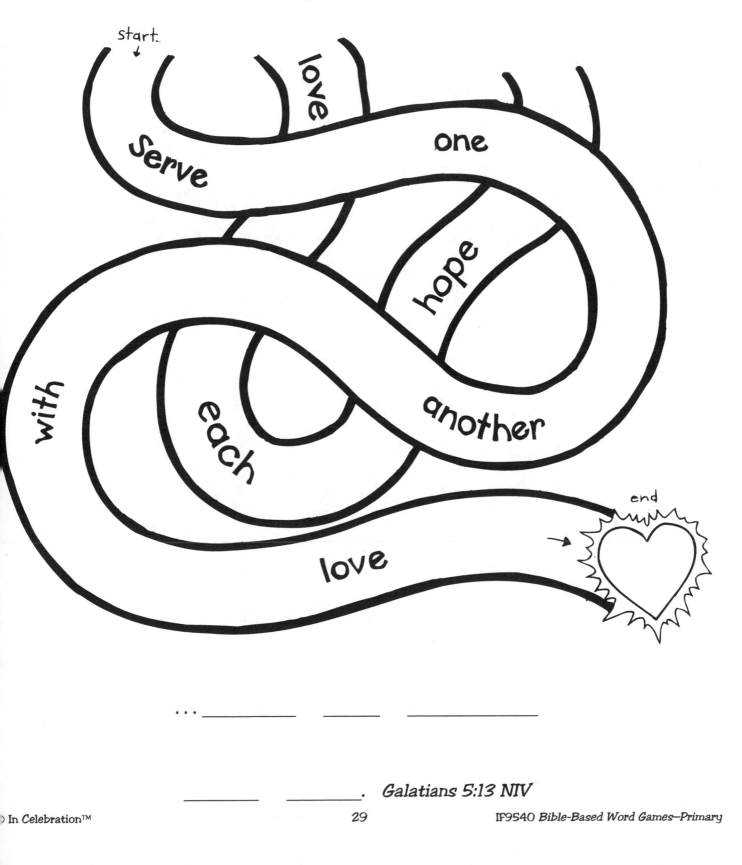

. . . _____ ____ _____

_____ _____. *Galatians 5:13 NIV*

Armor of God

Paul teaches us about the Armor of God.

Do you know what that armor is?

Write the letter that comes right before the letter shown in the alphabet.

You will learn about the Armor of God.

Ephesians 5

Answer Key

Page 4

```
    R A I N
    A
    N
    I        F
    M        L
  R A I N B O W
  N   L      O
P R O M I S E  D
  A
  H
```

Page 6

```
B M B L O O D D X A F
O F L I E S G A L B I
I F R W O G F R O W R
L V E O B Q L K C S S
S T U W G B O N U T T
H A I L Z S P E S A B
B P L Z G D E S T N O
R A D X W E I S S G R
S L I V E S T O C K N
```

Page 7

"...I am the Lord your God, ..."
"You shall have no other gods before me."

Page 9

Praise the Lord.

Page 10

Have I not commanded you?
Be strong and courageous. . . .
The Lord your God will be with you wherever you go.

Page 11

Therefore stand in awe of God.

Page 12

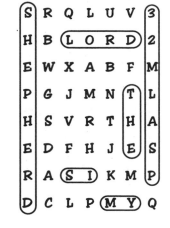

```
S R Q L U V 3
H B L O R D 2
E W X A B F M
P G J M N T L
H S V R T H A
E D F H J E S
R A S I K M P
D C L P M Y Q
```

Page 13

Shadrach
Meshach
Abednego

Page 14

He saw the spirit of God descending like a dove.
Matthew 3:16

Page 15

God can do everything.

Page 16

Greater love has no one than this,
that he lay down his life for his friends.

Page 17

Come follow me, . . .
and I will make you fishers of men."

Page 20

" . . .'worship the Lord your God,
and serve him only.' "

Page 21

" . . . love one another. . . ."

Page 22

Jesus said,

"Ask and it will be given to you;

seek and you will find;

knock and the door will be open to you."

Page 23

Page 24

Page 25

"You are the light of the world."

Page 27

I will call upon the Lord.

Page 28

Give Jesus your heart.

Page 29

. . . serve one another with love.

Page 30

RIGHTEOUSNESS

SALVATION

TRUTH

FAITH

WORD OF GOD

PEACE